LIVES AND TIMES

Dr. Seuss

Wendy Lynch

Heinemann Library
Chicago, Illinois

Designed by Visual Image
Illustrations by Sam Thompson
Originated by Dot Gradations
Printed and bound in Hong Kong/China

04 03 02 01
10 9 8 7 6 5 4 3

Library of Congress Cataloging-in-Publication Data

Lynch, Wendy, 1945-
        Dr. Seuss / Wendy Lynch.
            p. cm. – (Lives and times)
        Includes bibliographical references and index.
        Summary: A brief biography of the author of such books as "Green Eggs and Ham" and "The Cat in the Hat."
        ISBN 1-57572-216-X
        1. Seuss, Dr.—Juvenile literature. 2. Authors, American—20th century—Biography—Juvenile literature. 3. Illustrators—United States—Biography—Juvenile literature. 4. Children's literature—Authorship—Juvenile literature. [1. Seuss, Dr. 2. Authors, American. 3. Illustrators.] I. Title. II. Title: Doctor Seuss.

        PS3513.E2Z74 2000
        813'.52—dc21
        [B]   99-044283

Acknowledgments

The Publishers would like to thank the following for permission to reproduce photographs: Corbis: pp22, 23; Chris Honeywell: pp12, 14; Mandeville Special Collections Library, University of California, San Diego: pp17, 21; Yiorgos Nikiteas: pp18, 19; San Diego Union Tribune: p16; The Times: p20.

Cover photograph reproduced with permission of San Diego Union Tribune.

Every effort has been made to contact copyright holders of any material reproduced in this book. Any omissions will be rectified in subsequent printings if notice is given to the publisher.

Some words are shown in bold, **like this.** You can find out what they mean by looking in the glossary.

Contents

Part One

Theodor Seuss Geisel was born in Springfield, Massachusetts, on March 2, 1904. His parents called him Ted. His mother used to read stories and sing songs to Ted and his sister Marnie.

Ted's parents were German, so Ted spoke both German and English at home. His father used to take him to the park. Ted liked to visit the animals at the zoo there.

When he was five, Ted began to draw pictures of the animals in the zoo. He also began to read comic strips in the newspaper. His favorite was called "Krazy Kat."

At school, Ted liked to draw cartoons and write funny poems. In 1921, he went to **college**. Ted drew lots of cartoons for the college **magazine**.

In 1925, Ted went to Oxford **University** in England. Here, he met an American student named Helen. Two years later, they got married and moved to New York.

In New York, Ted began to work. He drew cartoons for **magazines** and for **advertisements**. Now he began to sign his name as Dr. Seuss.

In 1937, Dr. Seuss wrote his first children's book, called *And to Think That I Saw It on Mulberry Street*. It is about a boy who makes up stories about what he sees on his way home. Children liked the funny pictures in it.

In 1949, Dr. Seuss and his wife moved to a house called The Tower, in San Diego, California. Dr. Seuss had a **studio** there where he worked on drawing, painting, and writing books.

In 1957, Dr. Seuss wrote *The Cat in the Hat.* In the book, the Cat in the Hat made a lot of messes. Children loved it because it was funny and easy to read.

Dr. Seuss and his wife started a company
to make books that were easy to read.
In 1960, Dr. Seuss wrote *Green Eggs and
Ham*. It became his most famous book.

Dr. Seuss wrote and drew pictures for more than 40 books during his life. People liked the way the words **rhymed** and were **repeated**, as well as the funny pictures.

Would you like them here or there?

Dr. Seuss won many prizes for his books. In 1990, he wrote his last book, *Oh, the Places You'll Go*. He died on September 24, 1991, at the age of 87.

Part Two

There are many ways in which we can find out about Dr. Seuss. People took many photographs of him during his life. Here he is with one of his drawings.

Here are some pictures Dr. Seuss drew on his notes when he was at the **university**. He liked drawing better than studying.

You can read many books by Dr. Seuss. You can find them in bookstores or in a **library**. There may be some in your school library.

Books by Dr. Seuss can also be found on
CD-ROM. This means that you can read
his books or hear them read to you on a
computer. This shows how popular his
books are.

There have been many stories about Dr. Seuss in the newspapers. This story was written after he died. It tells about his life and the books he wrote. Many people were very sad when he died.

America mourns yooks, zooks and cats in hats

FROM MARTIN FLETCHER
IN WASHINGTON

AMERICA yesterday was mourning Theodor Seuss Geisel, alias Dr Seuss, the whimsical author and illustrator famous the world over for his cats in hats, fox in socks, scolding goldfish, yooks, zooks, grinches and nerds.

Mr Geisel died in his sleep at his California home on Tuesday night – a child of 87. The death last year of Jim Henson, creator of the Muppets, actually led the television news, but Mr Geisel's demise was considered almost as newsworthy in a nation so taken with fictional creations.

The passing of the man who invented green eggs and ham was prominently recorded on the front pages of almost every important newspaper. Experts in childrens' literature swiftly named him the Lewis Carroll of his generation. The newspaper *USA Today* even adapted his inimitable galloping rhythms to a versified editorial which began:

This is no time for fun,
This is no time for play.
Dr Seuss is no more,
It's a sad, sad, sad day.

Such was Mr Geisel's success and productivity that no two reports could quite agree on the bald statistics. Was it 48 books he wrote, or 49? Did they sell 100 million copies, or 200 million? Were they translated into 18, 19 or 20 languages? No matter. All agreed that the bow-tied Mr Geisel was the man who taught generations of children that reading could be fun.

He was born in Springfield, Massachusetts, in 1904 and had the run of the town zoo, his father being commissioner of parks. That evidently triggered his imagination, but it was not until 1936, after spells at Dartmouth College, Oxford University and as a commercial copywriter and illustrator, that he wrote his first book, *And to Think that I Saw it on Mulberry Street*, which was inspired by the rhythm of a liner's engines as he crossed the Atlantic.

Twenty publishers turned it down, but it became an instant best seller when it was finally printed.

He had no children, but two stepchildren by his second marriage, and told curious parents in typically self-deprecating style: "You make 'em. I amuse 'em." Mr Geisel's seemingly nonsensical books were fun, but often contained an underlying moral. The Lorax, one of his favourite creations, was an early environmentalist. *The Butter Battle Book* was a satire on the arms race.

Obituary, page 14

The Cat in The Hat, Dr Seuss's 1957 creation

Dr. Seuss drew many cartoons for the covers of **magazines**. You can still see these. Here is a cover he drew in 1932.

This library is at the **University** of California in San Diego. It has a room full of all sorts of things from Dr. Seuss's life. You can visit the library to learn about him.

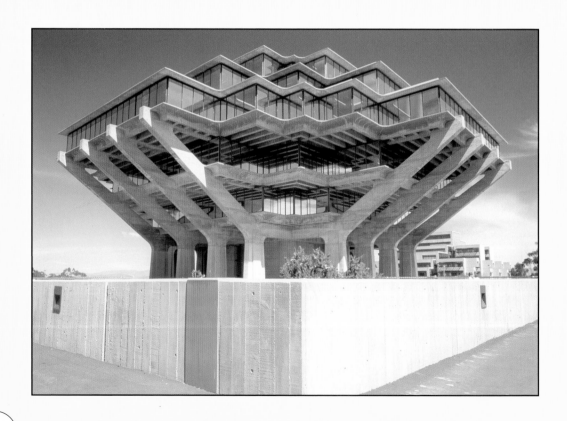

The **characters** in Dr. Seuss's books
are very popular. Here he is holding a toy
of the Cat in the Hat. Dr. Seuss will always
be remembered.

Glossary

This glossary explains difficult words, and helps you to say words which may be hard to say.

advertisement   picture or writing that tells people about a product. You say *ad-ver-tize-ment*.

CD-ROM   shiny disc that can store words, pictures, and music

character   person or animal in a story. You say *care-ak-ter*.

college   small school where people go to learn after high school

magazine   something to read that comes out every week or month

repeat   when something is said or written over and over again

rhyme   to end with the same sounds. You say *rime*.

studio   room to work in. You say *stew-dee-oh*.

university   very large college. You say *yoo-ni-ver-sit-ee*.

Index

More Books to Read

An older reader can help you with these books.

Weidt, Maryann N. *Oh, the Places He Went: A Story about Dr. Seuss.* Minneapolis: The Lerner Publishing Group, 1994.

Wheeler, Jill. *Dr. Seuss.* Minneapolis: ABDO Publishing Company, 1992.